THE HOW AND WHY WONDER BOOK OF
TREES

Written by GEOFFREY COE
Illustrated by CYNTHIA ILIFF KOEHLER
and ALVIN KOEHLER
Editorial Production: DONALD D. WOLF

Edited under the supervision of
Dr. Paul E. Blackwood, Washington, D. C.

Text and illustrations approved by
Oakes A. White, Brooklyn Children's Museum, Brooklyn, New York

WONDER BOOKS • NEW YORK

Introduction

Throughout the ages trees have inspired poets, provided themes for stories of fact and fiction, and served mankind in thousands of inspirational and practical ways. This *How and Why Wonder Book of Trees* clearly relates why these important plants have played such an essential part in the history of mankind.

Trees seem to have a special meaning for people everywhere. Who cannot think of a tree that has a special meaning or evokes a fond memory? Whether you think of trees as beautiful or ugly, helpful or bothersome, they are above all useful. They help us directly by providing food and shelter in hundreds of ways. In another hundred ways, they help us indirectly. They are homes for birds, beauty spots for recreational areas, and the source of endless lists of products from paper to pine tar.

To the scientist, trees are a source of information on how all plants live and grow. How does the basic life-giving chlorophyll help plants manufacture food? How do materials get from the soil and air into plants? How do the different parts of plants do their work? These are all questions for research — enough questions to keep scientists busy for a long time.

A walk in the woods or along a new street invariably brings out the question, *"What kind of tree is that?"* It's fun to be able to answer with the correct name of the tree. This *How and Why Wonder Book of Trees* provides descriptions that will be helpful in identifying many of the common trees in the United States. For those wishing to add to their collection of botany books, this will be a useful reference for home and school libraries.

Paul E. Blackwood

Dr. Blackwood is a professional employee in the U. S. Office of Education. This book was edited by him in his private capacity and no official support or endorsement by the Office of Education is intended or should be inferred.

Contents

SCRUB PINE

2 YR. OLD RIPE CONE

EGG CELLS
IN OVULES

SEED

POLLEN SACS

TYPICAL NEEDLES AND
CONE OF AN EVERGREEN

1 YR. OLD
CONES

The pollen of the male tree fertilizes the eggs in the ovules. The ovules are produced on scales of female cones.

GINKGO
(A LIVING FOSSIL)

LEAVES

LEAVES
WITH SMOOTH EDGES
(REDBUD)

LEAVES WITH TOOTHED EDGES
(HOP-HORNBEAM)

SIMPLE LEAF
(MAPLE)

PALMATELY COMPOUND
(HORSECHESTNUT)

ALTERNATE
(ELM)

PINNATELY COMPOUND
(BLACK LOCUST)

LEAVES
WITH LOBED EDGES
(SASSAFRAS)

BARK OF
SYCAMORE

BARK

BARK OF SWEET CHERRY

BARK OF HONEY LOCUST

WHAT TO LOOK FOR:

Everyone has seen trees. They are our largest plants. But do you know how to identify the kind of tree you are looking at? Trees differ in shape, leaves, bark, flowers and seeds. These are the things you have to learn to recognize.

There are two main groups of trees: 1. CONIFERS (evergreens). Various kinds of needles and cones are found on conifers. 2. BROAD-LEAVED TREES. Their leaves differ in size, type of edge, color, vein patterns, texture and arrangement on the stem. A *simple leaf* has only one leaf on a stem; a *compound leaf* has many leaflets on one stem. Some leaves grow opposite each other on the stem; others alternate, and some whorl. The veins of leaves have different arrangements that will help you distinguish the species or family of the tree.

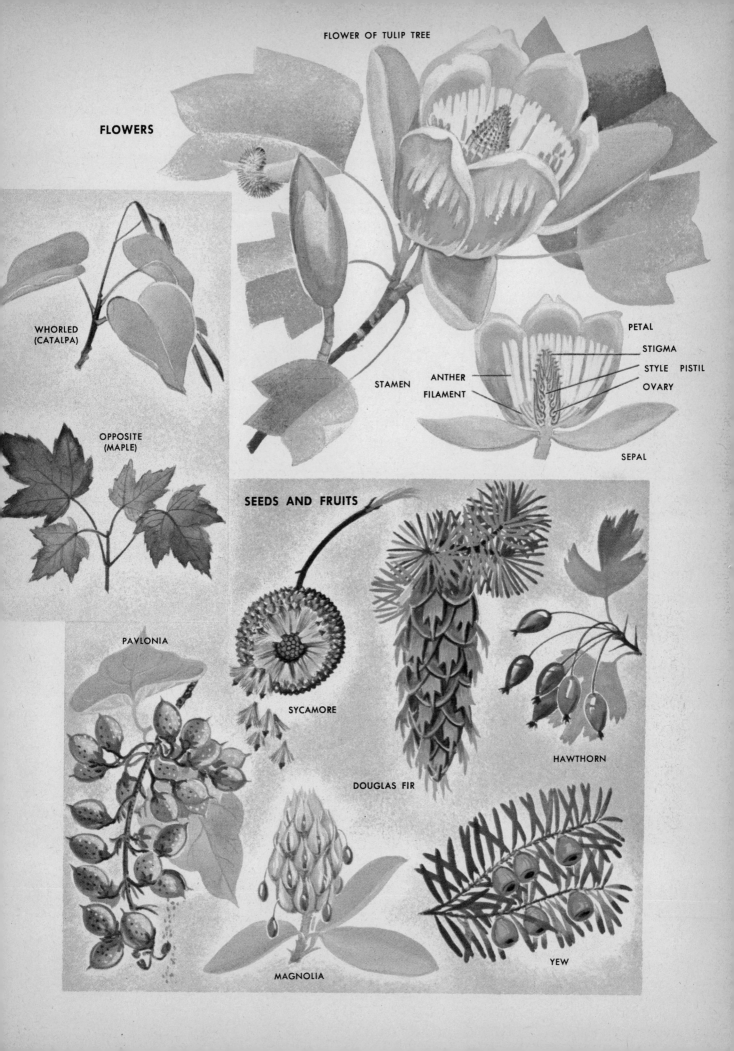

FLOWER OF TULIP TREE

FLOWERS

WHORLED
(CATALPA)

OPPOSITE
(MAPLE)

PETAL

STIGMA

ANTHER

STYLE   PISTIL

STAMEN

FILAMENT

OVARY

SEPAL

SEEDS AND FRUITS

PAVLONIA

SYCAMORE

DOUGLAS FIR

HAWTHORN

MAGNOLIA

YEW

The Ancestors of Our Trees

What is a tree?

A tree is many things.

It is a tall tower for small boys to climb to the top of, and look out over far horizons.

It is a songhouse for birds in the spring and summer; and in winter, when the birds are gone, the branches whistle in the chill wind.

It is a cool green umbrella to rest under on a hot summer day.

Its heavy trunk makes lumber for our houses, and finely grained wood for our furniture. Its limbs crackle merrily in our fireplaces at Christmastime.

Most of our houses have at least one tree standing nearby. Most boys have scrambled up trees and most girls have picked fragrant bouquets of peach or apple blossoms.

Trees are all around us, and they play an important part in our everyday lives. But, in a scientific sense, just what *is* a tree?

The dictionary defines a tree as "a woody plant, having a single stem or trunk, commonly more than ten feet in height, and a life cycle lasting more than two years." But like all rules, this definition has its exceptions. A few of the more curious of these exceptions are:

The amazing *banyan tree* grows in southern climates, and its long branches droop down and put roots into the ground until a single tree may have dozens or even hundreds of trunks. It resembles a small forest.

The *strangler fig,* whose windblown seeds germinate in the tops of other trees, and send down tendrils that take root all around the victim-tree and gradually smother it to death.

The tiny evergreens on the frozen tundra wastes of the north that grow only a few inches in a hundred years or more.

And, the exquisite little dwarf trees of Japan that look exactly like their giant cousins, yet are rarely more than a foot or two high.

But before we begin to discuss trees as we know them today, let us go back several million years in time and see how the first primitive ancestors of our modern trees developed.

Scientists estimate that our planet, Earth, is between four **How was the** and five billion years **soil created?** old. For most of that time, the earth had no soil at all. Dry land was nothing but barren rock. Then, slowly over the ages, the action of sun,

TREE   SHRUB   VINE

Trees, shrubs and vines are all woody plants, but there is a recognizable difference between the three: a tree has a definite trunk and grows, with few exceptions, 10 feet high or taller. A shrub is less than 10 feet high and has many stems rather than a single trunk. A vine has a weak stem and no crown like that of a tree.

wind and rain caused the thin top layer of the basic rock to crumble into sand and dust. About the same time, little plants from the sea water began to grow on rocks at the ocean's edge. Their tiny roots penetrated the rocks' surface and caused bits of it to scale off.

The plants, called *lichens,* died and decayed. Their remains mingled with the rock dust and gradually began to turn into soil. This primeval soil absorbed minerals from the rocks, the air, the plants, and the water. And thus the long process of soil building began.

As more and more primitive plant life took root and grew, it in turn withered and died; and the decaying vegetable matter continued to mix with the decaying rock to create even more soil. In this slow and tedious way, the layer of soil crept inland from the seashores until at last it formed a permanent carpet that covered virtually all of the earth's land surface.

You can see for yourself that the soil of our earth is nothing more than a mixture of decaying rock and decaying vegetable matter. Drop a handful of soil from your garden into a glass of water. Stir it up, and then let it settle. Some particles will float to the top. The rest will settle on the bottom. When you examine the floating particles, you will see that they are tiny bits and pieces of leaves and roots and other vegetable matter. The heavier particles that sink are sand and bits of gravel — the small remnants of weathered and broken rocks.

The soil nourishes all life on land. Without it, no vegetation can grow; and without vegetation, animal life could not exist. As the magic carpet of soil spread out over the earth's floor, the primeval plant life followed. At first, these little plants looked something like sea algae that had somehow managed to grasp a precarious roothold on the land. Then, as the soil carpet moved farther and farther inland, the plants grew larger and began to take on different forms.

How did land plants evolve?

Some of them grew deep roots to suck moisture and nourishment from the soil,

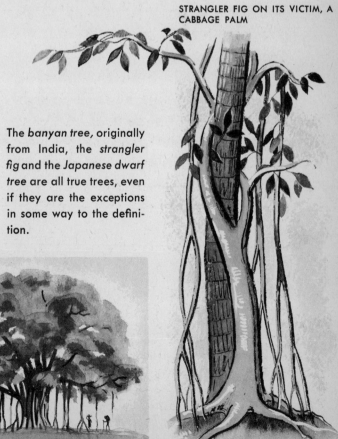

STRANGLER FIG ON ITS VICTIM, A CABBAGE PALM

The *banyan tree,* originally from India, the *strangler fig* and the *Japanese dwarf tree* are all true trees, even if they are the exceptions in some way to the definition.

JAPANESE DWARF TREE

BANYAN TREE

and developed leaves to absorb sunlight. These were the first ferns, and their form has changed little to this day.

As the eons dragged by in that early green but damp and dismal world, certain of these ferns grew to the size of huge trees, 100 or more feet in height. Others took on horsetail forms.. One type developed into what looked like gigantic asparagus plants, with heavy, swollen trunks and thick clusters of scale-like leaves on top. A few began to put out branches. And, after millions of years, the first true tree evolved. This was the *callixylon,* the ancestor of our modern conifers, or evergreens.

About 250 million years ago giant tree

How did early trees turn into coal?

ferns had emerged upon the landscape of the young earth; the evolution of the true trees had not yet occurred. This was an era known as the Carboniferous Period.

Most of the land at that time was wet and swampy, and as the tree ferns died and fell into primeval swamps, they were soon covered by mud and ooze. As time went on, layer upon layer of this decaying vegetation accumulated, each successive layer piling up on the one beneath it. Then pressures from inside the earth bent and buckled the earth's crust and forced the former swamp areas far underground. At the same time, these pressures compressed the plant material and formed it into the hard, black, brittle, flammable rock that we call coal.

Sometimes when a piece of coal is broken open, the fossil imprint of a fern leaf can be clearly seen, still as perfectly shaped as it was when it grew on the

ancient tree. It is from such relics found in coal, and in layers of fossil-bearing limestone and sandstone, that we are able to determine what the trees of the primitive world looked like.

Age followed age in that dim, distant

What were the earliest true trees?

time when the world was very young, and the surface of the earth and its climate changed with the passing of millions of years. Volcanic disturbances deep inside the earth buckled the rocky earth-crust and threw up towering mountain ranges. Many of the swamps and marshlands gradually gave way to hills and plains.

The great dinosaurs and other giant reptiles that had dominated early animal life died out and were followed by

FOSSIL BARK OF A SCALE TREE

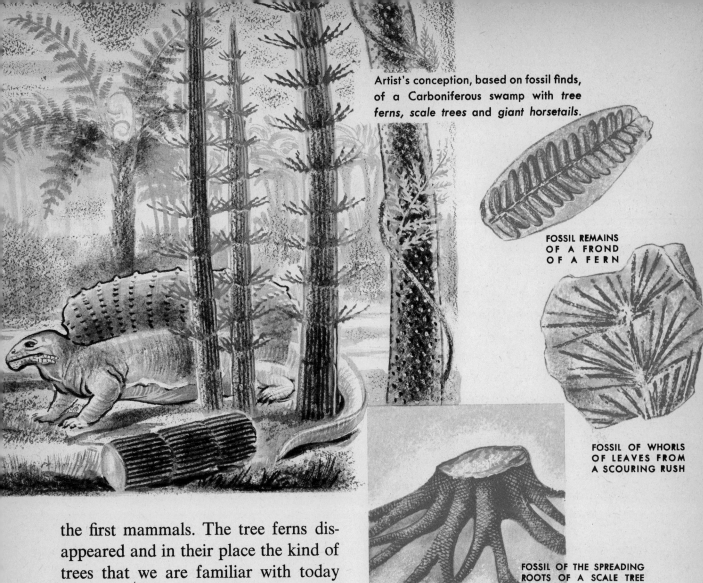

Artist's conception, based on fossil finds, of a Carboniferous swamp with *tree ferns*, *scale trees* and *giant horsetails*.

FOSSIL REMAINS OF A FROND OF A FERN

FOSSIL OF WHORLS OF LEAVES FROM A SCOURING RUSH

FOSSIL OF THE SPREADING ROOTS OF A SCALE TREE

the first mammals. The tree ferns disappeared and in their place the kind of trees that we are familiar with today began to develop. The first of these true trees were pines and palms. They were soon followed by hardwoods, which shed their leaves — willows, beech, oaks, maples, elms, and chestnuts. The earth's climate was much warmer then than it is today, and vast forests covered most of what are now the Arctic and Antarctic regions. Fruit trees and magnolias flourished in the lands now buried beneath the Greenland ice cap.

Then, for some reason which scientists still have not determined, the earth grew colder. The poles became shrouded in ice. Glaciers crept downward from the Arctic and covered most of Europe and about half of North America. When the glaciers finally receded about 20,000 years ago, they left the pattern of forests around the world very much as we know them today.

In the Petrified Forest of Arizona, and in other areas of **How were trees turned into stone?** the American West, there exist great fallen forests whose trees have turned to stone. Some of these tree trunks, which once were living Pines and Redwoods, are more than 100 feet in length. All of them lived, and died, 100 million years or more ago.

In that long-ago time, what is now the Western desert was a sub-tropical forest. Volcanoes belched their smoke and lava all around. Over the years, the great trees fell and were buried under the showers of lava ash. Then, gradually, the land turned into a swamp, and the trees were buried even deeper by accumulated layers of silt.

The water of these swamps contained a high percentage of dissolved quartz, which is one of the basic rock-forming minerals, as well as iron oxides. The water soaked into the cells of the wood; and, as the wood fibers decayed and rotted away, the quartz hardened into the same pattern as that of the original wood of the tree. So the petrified wood is not wood at all, but instead is composed of quartz crystals that have replaced the wood.

Eons later, as the climate of the region kept changing, the swamps dried out and became deserts; the erosive effect of the winds blew away the desert sand and uncovered the ancient trees.

MOUNTAIN ASH

Our Trees Today

How many kinds of trees are there? Although there are many thousands of different kinds of trees growing in the forested areas of our earth, all true trees are separated into two basic classifications. There are softwoods, sometimes called "evergreens" or "narrow leaved," and hardwoods, otherwise known as "deciduous" or "broad leaved." Of the two categories, only the hardwoods are flowering plants. The softwoods are conebearers.

The softwoods are the pines, firs, and others of the same family that usually have narrow needles instead of ordinary broad leaves. The term "evergreen" comes from the fact that these needles do not turn brown each autumn and fall to the ground, but remain green all winter long. Of course, the "evergreens" do shed their needles, but they do so a few at a time and not all at once at the approach of winter's frost. As a general rule, the wood of the pine or fir is softer than that of such broad-leaved trees as the oak or hickory; and thus they get their generic name, softwoods.

The hardwoods comprise all other true trees — such as the oak, the hickory, the chestnut, and the many other kinds that have broad leaves instead of needles. The word "deciduous" means that their leaves fall off the tree when autumn comes.

We have said earlier that most rules about trees have their exceptions. And here are two more. The larch, a true needle-bearing softwood, sheds all its needles every fall just as do the hardwoods. And in tropical climates, deciduous trees keep their leaves all year round because there is no annual frost to make the leaves wither and die.

SLIPPERY ELM

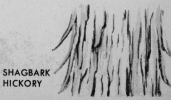

SHAGBARK HICKORY

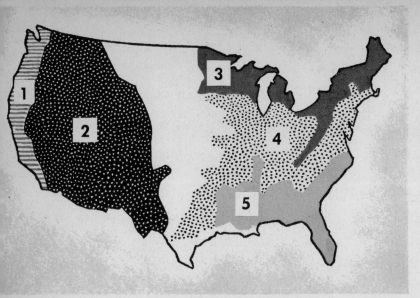

The United States can be divided into five distinct regions, each dominated by certain characteristic species of trees:

1. The west coast and redwood forests, with *redwood, Douglas fir, Engelman spruce, western red cedar, Joshua tree, Ponderosa pine, California laurel.* 2. The western forests, with *quaking aspen, western juniper, western larch, lodge-pole pine, Colorado blue spruce, piñon pine.* 3. The northern forests, with *black cottonwood, gray birch, mountain ash, bur oak, balsam fir, sugar maple.* 4. The central and southern hardwood forests, with *beech, tulip tree, elm, hemlock* and *shagbark hickory.* 5. The southern forests, with *American holly, live oak, Sabal palmetto, black gum* and *bald cypress.*

COTTONWOOD TASSELS

How did trees get their common names? Trees have always been so commonplace to man that, for the most part, they have been named for commonplace things. We all know the familiar trees that are named for the fruits or nuts they bear — apple, peach, pear, plum, orange, walnut, chestnut, pecan. Less well-known to most of us, perhaps, are the trees whose names came from the characteristics of their bark.

In the springtime, you can slip the bark off a slippery elm with only the pressure of your hand. Underneath is a sticky, gummy substance that is sweet to the taste, and is in fact used as a soothing ingredient in some cough medicines.

The bark of the shagbark hickory is so scaly and shaggy that it looks like the warped and weatherbeaten shingled roof of an old abandoned barn. The bark of the paper birch peels off in white sheets as thin as writing paper; that of the tanbark oak is used for tanning leather; and the bark of the toothache tree tastes so hot and peppery that, in pioneer days, it was chewed to relieve toothache.

Some trees are named for the color of their leaves or wood — the copper beech, the red oak, the blue ash, the white pine, the black spruce, to name only a very few. Sometimes this naming process is reversed. If we say that a thing is ebony in color, we mean that it is as black as the wood of the ebony tree; or if we say it is mahogany, we mean as dark brown as the wood of the mahogany.

A few trees derive their names from the place in which they are most likely to be found — the water oak, the river birch, the mountain hemlock, the western larch. Some are named for the qualities of their saps or resins — the sugar maple, the sweet gum, the pitch pine, the sourwood.

The pignut tree is a type of hickory which bears small, thin-shelled nuts that are relished by pigs. The cottonwood sheds soft cotton-like tassels that cover the ground beneath it with a white carpet. The sharp twigs of the pin oak were

PIN OAK TWIG

TANBARK OAK

PAPER BIRCH BARK

TREMBLING ASPEN

WEEPING WILLOW

sometimes used as wooden pins to take the place of nails in pioneer houses. The fever tree, of Africa, grows in low, swampy places that are usually unhealthy for human habitation.

The teardrop-shaped leaves of the trembling aspen quiver and shake in even the slightest breath of a breeze, so that the whole tree seems to be in constant motion. The thin branches of the weeping willow droop sadly to the ground as though in mourning.

Now and then, trees were named for men. The giant sequoia, largest and oldest of all trees, honors the great Indian chief, Sequoya; David Douglas gave his name to the great Douglas fir of our Pacific Northwest; and the magnolia was named for the French botanist, P. Magnol, who first transported seedlings from Louisiana to France.

To avoid confusion and to assure the possibility that someone in America knows what tree someone in France, for instance, is talking about, scientists have given trees Latin names, that are the same the world over.

THE PARTS OF A TREE AND THEIR FUNCTIONS

A single tree may produce several hundred thousands of seeds every year. The seeds of conifers are contained in the cones that hang sus-

How does a tree begin?

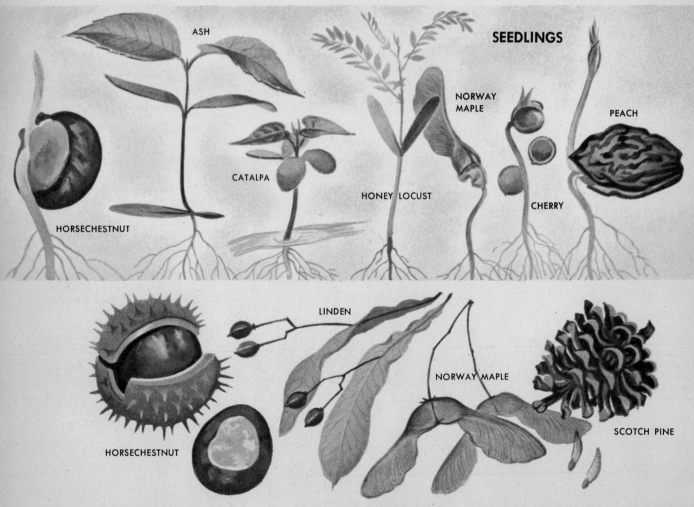

SEEDLINGS

ASH

CATALPA

HONEY LOCUST

NORWAY MAPLE

CHERRY

PEACH

HORSECHESTNUT

LINDEN

NORWAY MAPLE

SCOTCH PINE

HORSECHESTNUT

SEEDS AND SEEDCASES

PISTILLATE FLOWERS

COTTON-WOOD TASSELS

STAMINATE FLOWERS

SEEDS

Tree seeds vary from 27 per pound (buckeye) to 300,000 per pound (redwood). When conditions are right, seeds sprout and begin to grow.

SEED CASE

SEEDLING

ED CEDAR

PINE

HEMLOCK

MOUNTAIN MAPLE

BLACK OAK SAPLING

LEAVES

Make food for the tree by combining carbon dioxide from the air and water from the soil in the presence of sunlight.

HEARTWOOD

Core of inactive cells, formerly sapwood, which gives the tree strength and durability.

SAPWOOD

Sap rises through the cells from roots to crown. Food for seed production and for new tree growth is also stored here.

CAMBIUM

Layer of cells which divide and grow to produce a new layer of bark and wood between the old bark and wood each year.

INNER BARK

Food made in leaves moves down through these cells to branches, trunk and roots for growth and storage.

OUTER BARK

Protects trees from weather, insects, disease, fire and animals.

ANNUAL RINGS

Reveal age of tree.

By forming new cells under the bark and at the tips of the branches and roots, a tree grows in diameter, height and extent of root system each year.

GROWTH REGIONS

SOIL

WATER

ROOTS

Support the tree by penetrating the soil. Hold soil in place and conduct water and minerals to trunk.

ROOT HAIRS

Absorb water and dissolve minerals from the soil.

Birds are the most prolific seed distributors.

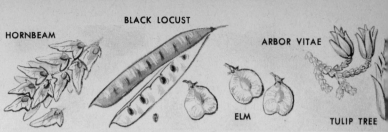

HORNBEAM

BLACK LOCUST

ARBOR VITAE

ELM

TULIP TREE

PAVLONIA

pended from their branches. Birches, willows and poplars produce their seeds on slender tassels. Apples and oranges contain several seeds inside each piece of fruit; peaches and plums have only one. The seeds of nut trees are the nuts themselves. Trees like basswood, cherry, and mountain ash bear seeds in berries; the locusts produce bean-like seeds in heavy pods. Each of these seeds contains all the essential elements needed to produce a baby tree. But usually less than one in a million survives to maturity.

To begin with, birds and insects eat most of the seeds while they are still on the tree. Squirrels and chipmunks live on the seeds of nut trees. Most of the remaining seeds fall on barren or rocky ground that is not favorable to their growth.

But since Nature distributes the seeds of trees with such a lavish hand, a few seeds out of all these millions manage to germinate and put out tiny roots. Then little leaves break through the ground and the young tree begins to grow. Yet even now, the odds are several thousand to one that it will ever develop into a full-sized tree.

The little sprouts crowd each other out in their fight for sunlight and for nourishment from the soil. Only the hardiest survive. And this ruthless competition keeps up even after many years of growth. The bigger trees overshadow the smaller ones and cut off their sunlight, and the smaller ones die. It has been estimated that in a single acre of natural pine woods, something like 5,000 trees die after they are twenty years old. When trees are planted by commercial growers, they are placed so that there is little or no such competition for life-giving sunlight.

How are seeds distributed? The wind is the greatest scatterer of seeds. The taller the parent tree, the better chance its seeds have for survival. Some seeds, notably the maple, are equipped with wings that spin like the blades of a helicopter. In a brisk breeze they can sail for several hundred yards from their parent tree and come to rest on new ground.

Birds are the most prolific seed distributors. After making a meal from the seeds of a tree, they scatter a few of them in their droppings over an area many miles wide. Deer often perform the same service when they eat wind-fallen apples. Squirrels frequently carry acorns to a hiding place, eventually forget about them, and the acorns take root and grow to become mighty oaks.

The most dramatic carriers of seeds

are the currents of the sea. Every coral island in the Pacific is fringed with groves of towering palms, which originally grew from coconuts that floated from the larger islands and the mainlands.

Regardless of how you place a seed in the ground when you plant it, part of the tree will grow downward into the earth to extract chemicals and water and the other part will grow upward into the air and sunlight.

Why do branches grow sideways?

The roots spread out in such a way as to find the most ground water. In the same manner, the branches grow sideways, all around the tree, in order to expose the maximum area of leaf surface to the sun.

At places where branches grow out from the trunk or from larger limbs, the tree's wood must be heavier and stronger to support the extra weight. This creates a knot in the tree, which we so often see as a swirl-like design in finished lumber.

The roots of a tree serve a double purpose. First, they provide a firm foundation that anchors the tree securely to the earth. Their second function is to absorb moisture from the ground and send it up-

Why does a tree have roots?

ward through tiny tubes, or veins, to the topmost branches and leaves.

On the average, the underground root spread of a tree is about one-tenth of the spread of its branches. In some species, particularly the oak, the root spread and branch spread may be nearly equal. The combined length of all the roots in a giant oak tree may total more than one hundred miles!

There are two kinds of roots: surface roots and tap roots. The tap root is an extension of the trunk that bores deep into the ground. The surface roots extend out on every side. All roots are covered with "hairs," as you can see for yourself, if you pull up a small seedling in the woods. From the soil, these "hairs" constantly absorb water mixed with a small quantity of nitrogen and other minerals in solution, and feed it to the body of the tree.

Tree roots also perform a valuable service to man. They bind the soil together and thus prevent it from washing away during heavy rainfalls. Moreover, they absorb vast quantities of water which, in a sustained downpour, might cascade down the slopes and carry off precious topsoil. A thickly-wooded river basin is good insurance against destructive floods and soil erosion.

In one respect, the roots of a tree behave in a way that appears to be contrary to most natural laws. They thrive best in soil that is poor and lacking in moisture. For this reason, they have to spread out farther and farther in order to collect enough water to feed the tree.

Seedling with roots, rootlets, root hair.

ROOT

ROOTLETS

ROOT HAIR

Winter tree bud: What will amount to a 10" or 12" growth, including flowers, is condensed into that small bud, of which you see a cross section at the left.

FLOWER

LEAF

HORSECHESTNUT

YOUNG CONES
OF NORWAY SPRUCE

You all have seen hardwood trees in bloom, but did you ever look at the beauty and colors of young cones?

FLOWERING MAGNOLIA

Under such circumstances, root tips behave almost as though they could think. Unerringly, they search out the pockets of soil most likely to contain moisture. If the root comes to a stone, it grows around it, and then continues on its determined path.

Because of this peculiar behavior of root tips seeking water, the great naturalist, Charles Darwin, suggested that a tree had the power to direct the movements of its parts in much the same manner as the brain of a lower animal such as the earthworm. Modern botanists know that a tree has no true nervous system; yet the leaves and branches, as well as the roots, respond to outside stimuli. Leaves tend to follow the sun in order to get as much light as possible. If a small tree has sprung up in the partial shade of a larger one, its branches try to extend themselves toward the sunny side.

Does a tree have a nervous system?

Trees have a complete circulation system, just as the human body has. Their sap acts in much the same way as blood. It flows up through veins from the roots to even the highest leaf, and then back down again to complete the circuit. The tree itself acts as a gigantic suction pump. A part of the water that reaches the leaves is evaporated by the air and sunlight. As the water in the leaves evaporates, it pulls on the water molecules nearest to it; they, in turn, pull on other water molecules, and so on, down to the very roots. Rain water cannot enter the pores of the leaves through which the tree's sap-water escapes. It can be absorbed by the tree only through the roots.

How does a tree pump water?

The water that does not evaporate through the leaves runs back down through the wood and bark of the tree. This is the true sap, and because it has picked up elements from the wood through which it has passed, it has more body than the water that is sucked upward. Thus, such saps as those of the maple or rubber tree are relatively thick and heavy.

A tree creates food for itself by an amazing chemical process known as *photosynthesis*. This term derives from two Greek words—*photos,* meaning "light," and *synthesis,* meaning "putting together." We are all familiar with such "synthetic" fabrics as rayon and nylon. Chemists create them by putting together different kinds of molecules and thus creating new atoms that become an entirely different substance. Basically, a tree does the same thing to make its own food. Stated in its simplest form, this is how photosynthesis works.

How does a tree feed itself?

VEIN PRINT OF OAK LEAF

Whereas animals inhale oxygen, a tree, like all plants, primarily inhales carbon dioxide. The tree breaks this down into component elements of carbon and oxygen. At the same time, it breaks down the water that comes from the roots into hydrogen and oxygen. Then *chlorophyll,* the mysterious substance that makes leaves and grass green, acts as a chemical agent. Using sunlight as energy, it combines the molecules of the water and carbon dioxide, and forms them into sugar, which is the food upon which the tree lives and grows. The process stops at night, when there is no sun.

Scientists have tried to duplicate the chemical processes that make the "leaf-factory" work, but without success.

We have seen that chlorophyll is the **Why do leaves change color?** magic substance that makes a leaf green. In cold weather, while the tree sleeps, the chlorophyll is not needed for its work of changing air and water into food-sugar. As the chlorophyll fades and the leaf begins to die slowly, other pigments become dominant and the leaf changes its color to yellows, reds and browns. Then, when the leaf is completely dead, it drops to the ground.

When the tree "wakes up" in the spring and begins to grow again, the new leaves are once more filled with green, life-giving chlorophyll.

Although a tree sucks in life-giving air **How does a tree breathe?** through its bark and branches and every other part, its chief "lungs" are its leaves. Each individual leaf is covered by a thin skin, and in this skin, on the underside of the leaf, are numerous tiny pores, called *stomata*. Through these minuscule stomata, the tree breathes in air and gives off the excess water vapor that is pumped up from the roots.

A tree is constantly inhaling air and exhaling moisture. This outflow of water vapor through the stomata of the leaves makes a large forest area moist and cool on a hot summer afternoon. A very large tree, such as an ancient oak, which may have more than half-a-million leaves, will discharge over 300 gallons of water into the air each day!

The bark of a tree serves much the same **Why does a tree have bark?** purpose as the skin of our bodies. The outside of the bark is thick and tough, and protects the growing parts of the trunk from insects, fungi, and other enemies.

The inner layers of the bark provide channels for food-sugar to flow downward from the leaves and furnish nourishment for the tree. Sometimes it also serves as a storage space for this food.

Since a tree grows in size by adding a layer of new wood to its circumference each year, the inner bark is constantly expanding to accommodate the growing trunk. The outer bark, being more or less dead, cannot expand. Instead it cracks and scales off, just as does the cuticle of the outer layer of human skin.

The outer bark of some big trees, such as the sequoia, may be as much as two feet thick. Extremely rich in tannic acids, it provides perfect protection against boring insects.

Cross section through leaf.

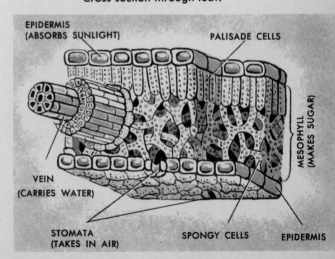

EPIDERMIS (ABSORBS SUNLIGHT)

PALISADE CELLS

MESOPHYLL (MAKES SUGAR)

VEIN (CARRIES WATER)

STOMATA (TAKES IN AIR)

SPONGY CELLS

EPIDERMIS

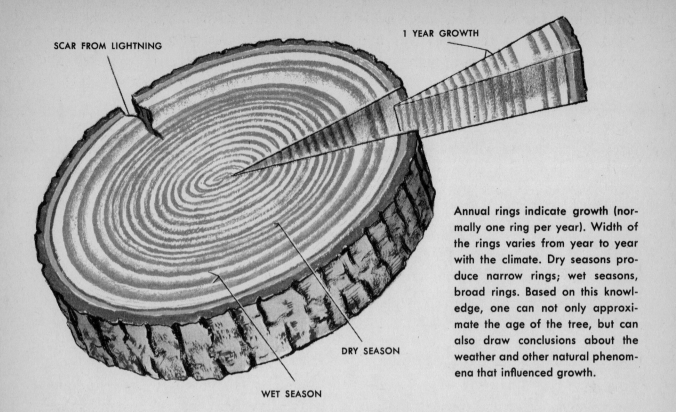

SCAR FROM LIGHTNING

1 YEAR GROWTH

Annual rings indicate growth (normally one ring per year). Width of the rings varies from year to year with the climate. Dry seasons produce narrow rings; wet seasons, broad rings. Based on this knowledge, one can not only approximate the age of the tree, but can also draw conclusions about the weather and other natural phenomena that influenced growth.

DRY SEASON

WET SEASON

THE AGE OF TREES

How does a tree show its age?

If you look at a cross section of a tree trunk, you will see that it is marked by a series of concentric rings. Roughly, these rings tell the tree's age. Each growing season, a tree adds a layer of new wood to its girth. During the cold months, when the sap ceases to flow, growth is temporarily halted and the tree rests. Thus the rings are clearly marked. By counting the rings, an expert can arrive at a reasonably accurate estimate of the tree's age.

When a tree trunk is sawed up into lengths of lumber, the pattern of the rings forms the "grain" of the wood.

The growth rings of very old trees can also tell us much about weather conditions in long-ago times. In periods of great drought, the rings do not grow as thick as in seasons when rainfall is plentiful. From that fact, scientific historians can piece together many secrets of the long-dead past. One of the most dramatic instances of this tree-ring history-book concerns the ancient cliff dwellers of southern Colorado.

About two thousand years ago, the cliff-dwelling Indians built villages high up on the sheer sides of canyon walls. In those days, the countryside of that part of Colorado was considerably greener than it is now, with sufficient rainfall to make agriculture possible. The Indians cultivated thriving farms on the tops of the mesas above their cliff towns. They also pastured their flocks of turkeys and goats there.

Then, in about the year 1276, more than two centuries before Columbus landed on the shores of the New World, a devastating drought struck the area. The crops withered and died. Grass

Left, *big tree*. Below, needles and cones of sequoia. Above, cones and needles from redwood.

REDWOOD

SEQUOIA

dried up, and the wild game left the country. Springs went dry, and the rivers that had cut out the canyons ceased to flow.

This period of drought and famine lasted for twenty-four years, and during this interval, the Indians abandoned their cliffside homes and migrated to new and more hospitable lands.

How can scientists be so sure of these dates and events? By a careful study of the growth rings of the ancient trees that survived!

The oldest living things on earth are also

What are the oldest trees?

— as would seem natural — the biggest. These are the giant redwood and sequoia trees of California.

Of the two, the redwoods are the taller — the loftiest specimen towering 368 feet into the sky. The sequoias are not as tall as the redwoods, but they are bulkier. The famous General Sherman tree is 273 feet high and 115 feet in girth, it is the largest living organism on the face of the earth.

The General Sherman began life as a seedling more than 3,500 years ago. Hundreds of other sequoias — some no more than fifteen or twenty feet in circumference — are from one to two thousand years old.

In Muir Woods, a carefully tended grove of giant redwoods only a few miles north of San Francisco, a cross sectional slab of an ancient tree is on display. The rings are marked to date

REDWOOD TREE

20

important historical events. One marked ring indicates the size of the tree at the time of the birth of Christ; others date the Norman Conquest of England in 1066, the landing of Columbus, the Revolutionary War. In the ring growths of this single tree, visitors can see the whole record of almost all recorded history.

It must not be supposed that the big trees of California are "living fossils." They are growing just as healthily in California forests today as they did 3,500 years ago. What might be called "baby" sequoias, perhaps 100 years old, are often not much bigger than ordinary Christmas Trees. In such parks as Muir Woods, you can buy tiny seedlings that could grow to become giant adults sometime in the 22nd century!

There is only one tree on record that authentically predates the sequoia and giant redwood in time. This was a specimen of bristlecone Pine that was discovered in California's White Mountains only a few years ago.

The ancient relic was short, gnarled, twisted and stunted. At the time it was cut by botanists in 1956, only a very small part of its trunk was still alive. This tree began its life on a stony mountain slope some 4,500 years ago. Throughout all its long existence, it was subjected to wintry blizzards, extreme periods of freezing cold, and short growing seasons. That it survived at all is a miracle. Scientists are now trying to determine whether or not other specimens of the bristlecone may approximate this weatherbeaten veteran in age.

But even though they may have to take second place to some bristlecone pines for old-age honors, the giant redwoods and sequoias will always reign as the undisputed monarchs of the world's forests — just as they have for the past 35 centuries!

ENEMIES AND DISEASES

From the time a seed falls from a tree, its struggle for life **What are a tree's enemies?** is a constant battle with the elements. We know that for every million seeds that fall, perhaps only one germinates and has a chance to grow. Then the little seedlings crowd each other out,

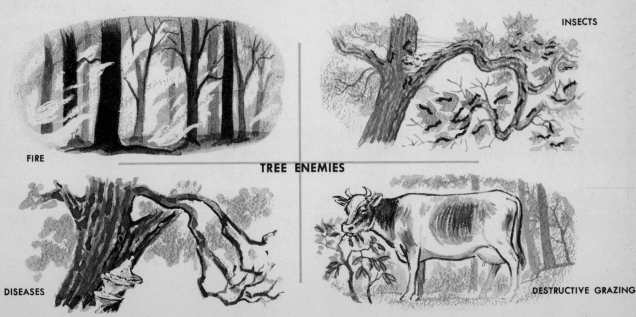

FIRE

INSECTS

TREE ENEMIES

DISEASES

DESTRUCTIVE GRAZING

21

vying for a place in the sun. Even after they have secured a firm foothold on life, most of the smaller trees are overshadowed and eventually killed by the bigger ones.

Aside from the constant competition for sunlight, winds, fire, and floods are the trees' most dangerous natural enemies. Many an old tree that has begun to rot with age finally goes down in a severe windstorm that younger, healthier trees can survive. And in fierce gales of hurricane intensity, thousands of young and vigorous trees are uprooted and fall.

Fire is the most dramatic destroyer of the forest. Most fires are caused by lightning. But in recent years, with more and more people driving through forest preserves, many destructive fires

LEAF-CHEWERS

have been caused by careless campers and smokers.

Only the big trees of California, like the sequoias, seem to be nearly invulnerable to lightning. Most of the larger ones have been struck time and time again by lightning bolts, and bear the visible scars of such encounters. But a flash that would shatter even the mightiest of oaks, will be taken in stride and shrugged off by the sequoia.

What are the insect enemies? There are many thousands of kinds of insects that live in the forests and feed upon the trees. Like all of Nature's creatures, these insects play their part in the cycle of life. Some carry pollen from one flowering plant to another. Others eat the dead and decaying wood that falls to the ground, and thus keep the forest floors clean. Most, in turn, are eaten by birds and small animals — and in doing so pass on the basic energy of life converted by chlorophyll from the sun, air, and water.

WOOD EATERS

TWIG BORERS

For the most part, these forest insects do little or no permanent damage to trees. But under certain circumstances, they can become killers. For the sake of simplicity, we can divide these potential killer-insects into five general types.

The *leaf chewers* live on the leaves of a growing tree and munch endlessly as they crawl slowly along. Ordinarily, they do no damage, for a healthy tree produces many more leaves than it requires for breathing or food-making. In some seasons, however, unusual numbers of these insects make their appear-

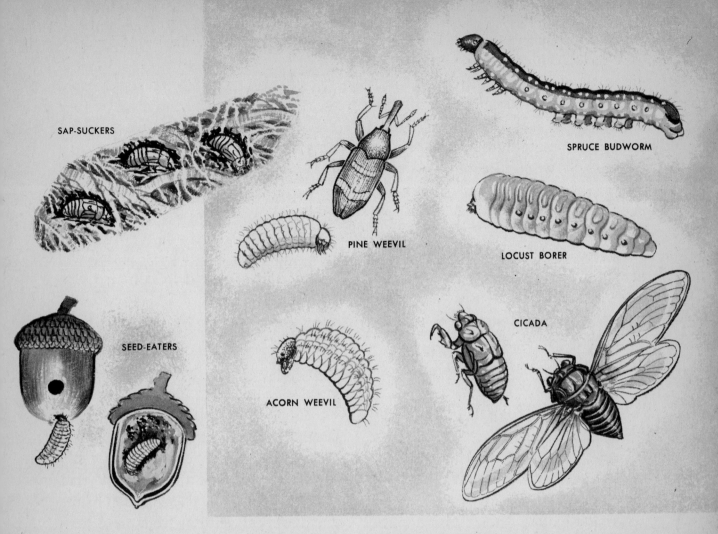

SAP-SUCKERS

PINE WEEVIL

SPRUCE BUDWORM

LOCUST BORER

SEED-EATERS

ACORN WEEVIL

CICADA

ance. When this happens, so much of the total leaf area of a tree is eaten that the tree literally starves to death. On such occasions, in "bad insect years," whole forests have been wiped out.

The *twig borers* eat their way into the twigs and smaller branches. By killing a large part of a young tree's crown, the general growth of the whole tree is stunted. The afflicted tree is then overtopped by neighboring trees, its source of sunlight is cut off, and it dies.

The *wood eaters*, equipped by Nature with strong jaws and mouths, tunnel into the living fiber of the tree's trunk. Not only do they destroy the veins through which the tree gets its life-giving sap, but they also weaken the tree structurally so that it is more easily

Leaf-chewing insects are predominantly the larvae of butterflies, moths, beetles and sawflies. One of the most devastating is the *spruce budworm,* the caterpillar of a moth.

Twig-borers are practically all larvae of beetles, with the *pine weevil* as a typical example.

Wood-eating insects, equipped with strong biting and chewing mouth parts, are usually found in the beetle group, both adults and larvae. One is the *locust borer,* the larva of a black and yellow longhorned beetle.

Sap-sucking insects are found among the aphids, cicadas, tree-hoppers and spittlebugs. The largest of them are the cicadas.

Seed-eating insects are the larvae of some species of wasps, beetles and moths. We give the *acorn weevil* as a typical example. (The adult drills a hole into the seed and deposits the eggs.)

blown over and destroyed in a heavy windstorm.

The *sap suckers* feed on the life blood of the tree. As is the case with the leaf chewers, they normally cause no per-

23

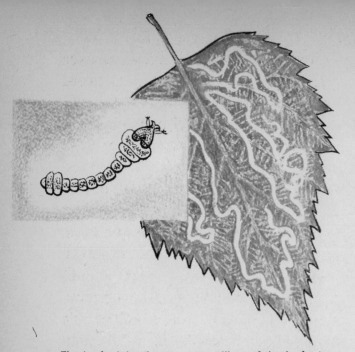

The leaf-mining insects, caterpillars of the *leaf-miner moths,* are flat enough to tunnel through the leaf tissues. Their trails look like some strange kind of writing on the leaf. They are often smaller than a pinhead.

manent damage. But if exceptionally large numbers appear in the forests in a given season, they may drain the sap of its vitality or even poison it. They may also pass along disease from tree to tree, and thus wipe out whole forest populations.

The *seed eaters,* like most other forest insects, rarely do great or lasting damage. A tree produces seed in such lavish plentitude that those eaten by these little creatures are never missed in Nature's scheme of things. But again, in certain years, the seed eaters appear in such vast numbers that virtually the whole seed crop of certain trees is destroyed. This, of course, affects entire forested areas by eliminating the new growth of trees for a full season or more.

There are chiefly two kinds of tree diseases. One is

What are the diseases of trees?

caused by viruses that are small primitive organisms that are generally passed from tree to tree by insects like the sap suckers. The other, the principal cause of tree disease, are various kinds of fungi. Fungus spores can be carried from one tree to another by insects, wind, water, or birds. Of the two, the fungi are the more destructive to the world's forests.

Two of the most tragic of American tree epidemics were visited upon the American elm and the chestnut — seriously threatening the existence of the former and almost entirely wiping out the latter.

The American elm was attacked by both a virus and a fungus disease almost at the same time. Between the two enemies, elms began to die at an alarming rate throughout almost all of the eastern United States. Tree experts rushed to the rescue of this fine old American tree, and there is hope that the disease may be checked before the elm disappears entirely from the American scene as did the chestnut only a few years before.

There was no such hope for the chestnut. Attacked by a fungus, it was practically wiped out before anything could be done to save it.

Almost every grandparent will re-

member the luxuriant stands of chestnut trees that once dominated the eastern United States. One of the favorite childhood sports of the 1920's was gathering great sackfuls of the thorny fruits, pounding off the outer burrs, and then roasting the sweet inner nuts over a roaring fire. Then a rare fungus disease was accidentally introduced from Asia, and within the space of a year or two, the lordly chestnut trees withered and died. Nothing was left of them but dead trunks that soon toppled over and mingled their remains with the forest floors.

But, happily, the chestnut seems to be refusing to die altogether. Sometimes, when you are walking through the woods, you will see new chestnut shoots growing out of a long-dead stump. The deadly fungus is still present in our forests, and continues to attack the young shoots as they bravely spring up and try to grow. But perhaps, in time, enough of them will develop an immunity to the disease so that once again we will have healthy chestnut trees. Perhaps your children will be able to go into the woods on a "chestnut hunt" just as your grandparents did.

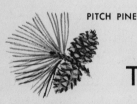

PITCH PINE

HICKORY

Trees of the American Woods

When the first settlers came to America from Europe, the country they found was covered with a vast green forest of virgin trees. In most places these woods were all but impenetrable, pierced only by narrow animal paths and blazed Indian trails. The Indians made little real use of the forest that grew so profusely all around them. They gathered dried, fallen twigs for their fires and huts. They peeled the thin, waterproof bark from birch trees to cover their canoes. They cut straight, stout branches of ash, hickory, and other tough, resilient woods for their bows and arrows. They used the thin, stringy root of the larch as thread. They planted their small gardens of corn and beans in natural clearings, or in areas that had been burned out. But rarely did they have occasion to cut down the giant trees of the primeval forest.

What did the settlers find?

With the coming of the white man to America, however, the face of the woods began slowly to change — never

In summer, the birch bark canoe was the main means of transportation for the Eastern Woodland Indians.

to return to its original glory. To the settler, the vast growth of trees was a nuisance; and he got rid of them as rapidly as he could.

He cut down large areas of trees to clear his fields, and burned the fallen timber in great bonfires. He used the trunks of smaller trees for his cabins, and split it up into planks to make his furniture. As the settlers moved westward, the grand virgin forests disappeared behind them. Only a few scattered groves of the original trees were left standing in their wake.

Yet in the two or three centuries since the white man invaded the American woods and despoiled them of their magnificent trees, much of the woodland has come back in the form of second- or third-growth timber. As you stroll through segments of the American woods today, here are some of the most common — as well as the most beautiful — trees that you will see.

THE EVERGREENS

Evergreens are the most numerous trees north of the equator. Certainly they are the most valuable from a commercial standpoint — for building-materials, paper, and turpentine and other resin products. Sometimes evergreens make up great forest areas exclusively. In other places, they are interspersed with stands of hardwoods. In New England, for example, evergreens are likely to be found on the lower slopes of the mountain ranges, hardwoods on the heights of the ridges.

Speaking broadly, evergreens fall into six general categories: pine, spruce, fir, hemlock, cedar, and larch. Evergreens are called "conifers" because they bear fruit in the form of cones, which are comprised of thin wooden disks laid one on top of the other. The one exception to this is the cedar, most types of which bear their seeds in berries instead of cones.

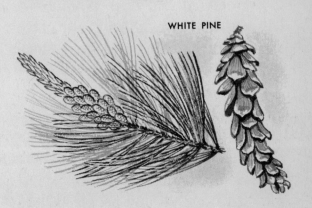

WHITE PINE

White pine is the giant timber tree of the American Northeast and the Great Lakes country. Growing straight and strong to heights up to 100 feet, its trunk was used as the masts and spars of the famed New England sailing ships. Its timber was so prized for building, not only for house frames but also for floors and paneling, that early lumber companies cut it ruthlessly and all but wiped it out. Like all of America's timber resources, white pine is carefully conserved today under U. S. Government supervision.

PINE   SPRUCE

NORWAY PINE

Norway pine (also called red pine) is found in about the same geographical area as white pine, although isolated forests of it grow as far south as northern West Virginia. It, too, is extremely valuable as a timber tree.

No one is quite sure how this native American tree came to be given the name "Norway." Many people believe that early settlers mistook it for a species of spruce that grows in Norway.

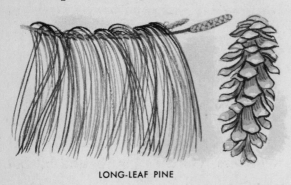

LONG-LEAF PINE

Long-leaf pine is distinguished, and easily recognizable, by its clusters of extremely long needles that grow from 12 to 18 inches in length. It grows from 100 to 120 feet high in the southeastern states from Virginia to northern Florida. Long-leaf is valued for its fine timber and, along with a very close relative, slash pine, it is the principal source of turpentine and pine tar. As you drive along the highways in southern states, you will see large forests of long-leaf pine. Each tree has a small bucket affixed under diagonal cuts in the bark to catch the valuable sap.

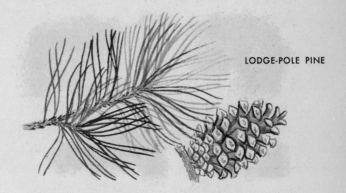

LODGE-POLE PINE

Lodge-pole pine is a relatively small species in a land of usually tall trees. Its foliage is sparse, and so it grows in stands where the individual trees are fairly close together. For this reason, the ground underneath these groves is generally bare of anything but dead branches and a brown carpet of fallen needles. Western Indians used the straight trunks of the smaller of these trees as poles for their tepees and lodges. Thus it was named "lodge-pole."

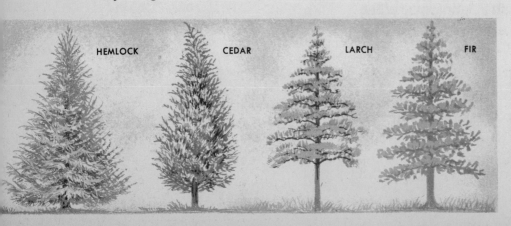

HEMLOCK   CEDAR   LARCH   FIR

Speaking broadly, evergreens fall into six general categories: pine, spruce, fir, hemlock, cedar and larch.

27

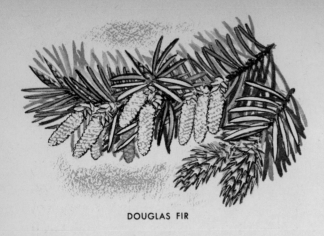

DOUGLAS FIR

Douglas fir, sometimes called "Oregon pine" by lumbermen, is the most valuable of all the timber trees in America. Next to the giant redwood it is the tallest of all trees, many big ones towering more than 200 feet. Douglas fir yields all sorts of building material from plywood to construction timbers. When the smaller trees are thinned out of the forests to give the larger ones more growing room, tens of thousands are sold as Christmas trees.

BALSAM FIR

The *balsam fir,* a near relative that grows in the northeast, is the favorite Christmas tree of the eastern part of the country. Its boughs are especially springy and fragrant. Underneath the bark of this big tree are little pools of resin. Known as "Canada balsam," this resin is so pure that it is used for mounting specimens in laboratories.

The third major source of Christmas trees is the *spruce.* But far more important from the economic point of view is the fact that the several kinds of spruce furnish most of our pulp-wood for paper making. It has been estimated that more than 100 acres of spruce forests must be harvested to make enough paper for a single edition of the *New York Sunday Times* alone. From such a figure as this, it is easy to understand why the careful "tree farming" of spruce is one of the major projects of our government's Conservation Service.

NORWAY SPRUCE

Hemlock is a tall, graceful tree that grows both in the Northeast and the Northwest. Compared to the pines, its wood is not much good for timber, and so it was largely passed over by the early lumbermen. As a result, many of the original stands of this fine old tree are intact today. Hemlock is hardy and is easily transplanted. For this reason, small hemlocks are planted as decorative hedges and can be easily kept trimmed into shape.

HEMLOCK

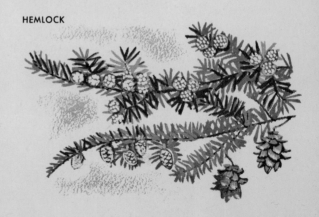

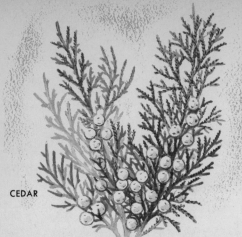

CEDAR

Cedars are found in most of the entire eastern half of the United States, and can be quickly distinguished from other evergreens. The needles are extremely short, and the foliage is so dense and compressed together that the whole tree looks like a solid object.

The cedar's wood is a delicate shade of red and delightfully aromatic. While it smells good to humans, it is offensive to moths and they refuse to go near it. So cedar is used to make clothes chests and as a lining for closets. A fragrant oil, distilled from the wood and needles, is distilled into an ingredient used in furniture polish. The wood of the white cedar is so water- and decay-resistant that it is used for roofing-shingles and fence posts.

Juniper is a type of cedar found largely in the West, where it prospers in arid, rocky, sandy soil. The tiny needles exude a fragrant resin that fills the hot

JUNIPER

desert air with a delightful perfume. Juniper berries provide food for some small types of wildlife.

Larch, sometimes called by its Indian name "Tamarack," is one of the few conifers that sheds all its needles at the approach of winter, leaving its long, drooping branches bare and brown. Yet even with the needles gone, the larch still presents the symmetrical appearance of an evergreen, and its small cones do not drop when the leaves do. Larches are usually found in low damp places, but they grow almost equally well on fairly high ground.

LARCH

Bald cypress is the big tree of the southern swamps, where it grows in the water. Unlike most swamp vegetation, the cypress grows straight and tall, as much as 100 feet high. At its base, the trunk flares out like a bottle, Nature's way of lowering the tree's center of gravity so that the tall trunk will be supported in the gummy swamp mud and ooze.

Curious little conical projections, called "knees," — part of the cypress's root system — jut up out of the water all around the base of the trunk, their tips just above the water level. The purpose of these "knees" is to provide ad-

BALD CYPRESS

ditional air to the roots. The roots of ordinary trees would be able to get this air from spaces in the loose soil around them.

Like the larch, the cypress sheds its leaves each fall, even though most of them grow in Florida and along the southern Gulf Coast where frosts only rarely occur. And like the live oak, whole forests of these swamp giants are draped and festooned with decorative streamers of moss.

THE HARDWOODS

The *oak* is perhaps the commonest tree found in the American woods, and there are more different kinds of oaks growing in various parts of the country than any other type of tree — white oak, black oak, red oak, scarlet oak, pin oak, scrub oak, and post oak to name only a few. All of them are strong, solid trees that usually grow to a great size and live to a ripe old age. "Sturdy as an oak" is a common descriptive

phrase used to denote exceptional strength.

The leaves of oaks come in varied shapes and sizes, but all oaks have one thing in common: all bear acorns. Whenever you see an acorn, you can be sure that the tree is an oak, regardless of how unfamiliar the leaves may seem.

One of the most magnificent of all oaks is the *live oak* of our southern states. It is so called because it does not shed its leaves in the fall but keeps them all year around. Another peculiarity of the live oak is the profusion of Spanish moss that festoons its branches. This Spanish moss is not a true moss at all but an odd parasitic growth that, curiously enough, is related to the pineapple family. If any one tree characterizes the Deep South, it is the moss-festooned live oak.

The *maple* is generally considered to be America's most beautiful tree. Unlike most other broad-leafed trees, its branches grow in nearly perfect symmetry. In early fall, when its leaves begin to turn, it brightens the woods with vivid splotches of red, yellow, and orange. (See page 32.)

In addition to its beauty, the maple is one of the most useful of trees. Its

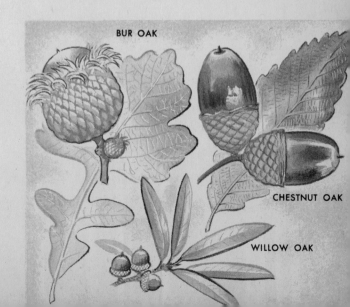

BUR OAK

CHESTNUT OAK

WILLOW OAK

finely grained wood has always been highly prized by furniture makers; and the syrup made from its sweet sap is an American breakfast-table delicacy.

Although they vary slightly, the leaves of the several kinds of maples look similar, and easily identify the tree. Common to all maples, too, are the delicate winged seeds that sail through the air like flights of tiny airplanes in the early-summer breeze.

The *locust* took its name from a story in the Bible. The New Testament tells us that John the Baptist lived in the wilderness on locusts and wild honey. Even though it is true that many kinds of insects are eaten by the people of the Near East, early Bible readers rebelled at the idea of John actually enjoying a locust diet. So they decided that what he probably had eaten were the sweet seeds of the carob tree. Therefore, they named a similar podbearing tree the locust.

The seeds of the *honey locust,* which are encased in long pods, are very sweet, and were eaten in pioneer days as candy. These pods, and the long multiple leaves, are the identification marks of the locust. The wood of the black locust is extremely hard and durable.

It is most commonly used to make fence posts and railroad ties. (See page 32.)

The *willow* often grows along river banks or on the sides of ponds. Although classified as a "hard wood" tree, its wood is very soft and is rarely used for lumber. While the trunk of an adult willow is heavy and gnarled, its upper branches are so light and thin that they droop downward and sometimes break off from their own weight.

The twigs of a willow can perform the same function as its seeds. If you put a willow twig in soft, damp ground, it will take root and start putting out leaves. When you see a long line of willows along a river, it is often because twigs have fallen off a parent tree, been carried downstream by the current, and then taken root along the bank. (See page 32.)

The *sycamore,* one of the stateliest of trees, grows to great heights. An old specimen often towers 100 feet or more.

The most notable feature of the sycamore is its colorful, mottled bark which mixes patches of gray, white, light green, and light brown like the pattern of a quilt. Botanists think the sycamore was the first hardwood tree to develop on earth. (See page 33.)

The sycamore's leaves look very much like the maple's, except that they are larger and wider. The seeds are contained in round balls about the size and general appearance of golfballs. They dangle down from the upper branches as though tied on with strings. In some parts of the country, sycamores are called plane trees or buttonwoods.

The *sweet gum,* another tall tree of the southern woods, often attains a

RED OAK

BLACK OAK

MOSSY CUP

LIVE OAK

There are more different kinds of oaks than any other type of tree.

31

stature of 100 feet or more. It has leaves like five-pointed stars, seed-balls very much like those of a sycamore, and its thick bark exudes a heavy, sweet resin that country children chew as chewing gum. (See page 33.)

The *magnolia* is a lush and beautiful flowering tree that is native to the South. In its natural habitat, it grows in the damp, loamy soil of river banks and marshy places; but in many Southern cities it has been planted as a lovely streetside ornament. (See page 33.)

Its leaves are heavy and shiny. They feel almost like polished leather and gleam brightly in the sun. Its flowers are huge, creamy white or light pink, and grow on the tree almost as profusely as roses on a rosebush. When they are in full bloom, they perfume the air all around with a heavy fragrance.

Other trees of the magnolia family, all with similar characteristics of leaves and flowers, are the *umbrella tree*, the *cucumber tree*, and the *sweet bay*. The first two are found in the woods of the Allegheny Mountain area, from Maryland and West Virginia southward. The sweet bay grows along the coastline from Florida as far north as Boston. Generally, all three are referred to as magnolias.

The *tulip tree,* sometimes called the yellow poplar, is also of the magnolia family. It is the family's giant big brother. Some specimens grow from 90 to 120 feet tall. Its flowers are shaped like tulips, which give this tree its name.

The *flowering dogwood* is one of America's most spectacular trees. Early in the spring, even before such early-budding trees as the maples begin to green up, the dogwood suddenly bursts out in a blaze of glorious color. There are two kinds, white and pink. The white is the wild tree; the pink is a cultivated variety. But the two colors are so frequently interspersed that they create a delightful pattern on the otherwise bare spring hillsides. (See page 33.)

RED MAPLE

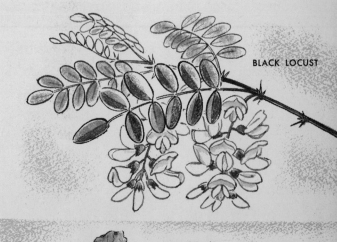

BLACK LOCUST

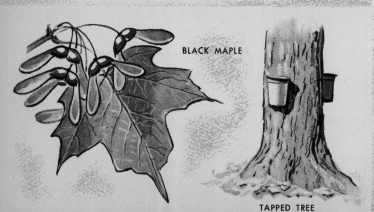

BLACK MAPLE

TAPPED TREE

PUSSY WILLOW

SYCAMORE

SUGAR MAPLE

SWEET GUM

HAW

DOGWOOD

JUDAS TREE

SWEET BAY

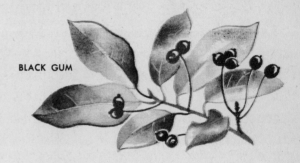

PISTILLATE

YELLOW BIRCH

STAMINATE

Birches, which grow in the cooler parts of the Northern Hemisphere, have attractive foliage, slender, tassel-like catkins which bear pollen, and a fine-grained hard wood used for furniture.

The *ash* has multiple leaves, like the locust, and winged seeds like the maple. But the seeds of the ash have only a single wing while maple seeds have two. Like many trees, the several kinds of ash are named for colors — white, black, blue, red, and green. Yet, like the maples, it is difficult for anyone except an expert to tell them apart.

WHITE ASH

The *black gum,* also called sour gum and tupelo, is not related to the sweet gum. Instead, it belongs to the dogwood family. Only about half as tall as the sweet gum, its trunk grows straight up, hardly varying in circumference from bottom to near the top. Its branches and twigs jut out almost horizontally. Its oval leaves are smooth and shiny,

and in the fall they turn a brilliant red, appearing almost as flashing spurts of flame in the midst of the thick woods.

BLACK GUM

The *sassafras* was called green stick by the Indians because of its bright green twigs. The Indians also liked to chew the tender, aromatic bark of the twigs, just as children living in the country do today. An old-time folk remedy, sassafras tea, is made from the roots. Many rural doctors still prescribe it as an all-around tonic.

SASSAFRAS

THE FRUIT TREES

In song and legend, as well as in fact, the *apple* is the most famous and most numerous of all our fruit trees. Apples were the first trees brought to America by the original settlers, and the first trees carried westward in covered wagons by the pioneers.

According to Biblical legend, an apple was the fruit used by Satan to tempt Eve in the Garden of Eden. King Solomon sang: "Comfort me with apples." When an apple fell from a tree and hit Sir Isaac Newton on the head, it started in his mind a trend of thought that resulted in the laws of gravitation.

One of the most colorful folk-characters of early American history was Johnny Appleseed, a kindly old man who is said to have wandered up and down the Ohio Valley planting apple trees wherever he went. The curious thing is, though, that when seeds from even the finest varieties of apples such as Delicious, Baldwin, and Rome Beauty are planted, they yield small, sour fruit that is not very good to eat. Apple trees must be grafted to produce good fruit; that is, they must be reproduced through the wood instead of the seed. So maybe Johnny Appleseed planted cuttings instead of seeds.

Apple trees are very susceptible to disease, and must be constantly sprayed to keep yielding good fruit. Only young trees produce choice fruit, and, in commercial orchards, the older trees are cut down to make room for new ones. But the old patriarch trees, twisted and gnarled, bursting with delicate pink blossoms in the springtime, are the favorite decoration of almost every rural farmyard.

CHERRY

PEACH

PEAR

Cherries, peaches, and *pears* are America's next most popular fruits. Like the apple, they probably originated somewhere in the Near East. Also like the apple, they produce blossoms in the spring that are as pleasing to the eye as their fruits are delicious to the taste.

Cherry wood is considered one of the finest of all materials for furniture. It is smooth, rich in color, finely grained; and its beauty improves with age. Wild cherry grows profusely in woods east of the Mississippi.

The *persimmon* is a peculiar wild fruit tree that flourishes from the middle South to Florida. It is invariably associated with the possum, because when the fruit is ripe it is that funny little animal's favorite delicacy. People who like to eat possum meat usually know where to find some if there are persimmon trees around. Persimmon fruits look like small green apples; but until they have been touched with frost, beware of biting into one! It contains a powerful astringent acid that will pucker up your mouth as painfully as if you chewed a piece of alum.

But the first frost ripens the persimmon, and then it is one of the most delicious fruits that grows. Its scientific name, *Diospyros,* means "food of the gods." Amazingly enough, the persimmon tree is a distant relative of the tropical ebony.

The *citrus* fruits — orange, lemon, lime, and grapefruit — are grown chiefly in Florida and California, for the trees cannot withstand heavy frost.

CHERRY

PEACH

PEAR

APPLE

ORANGE

LEMON

TANGERINE

GRAPEFRUIT

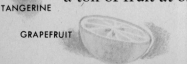

Like most American fruit trees, the original species came from the Middle East and were imported into this country by way of Spain and the West Indies. In fact, Columbus brought the first oranges and lemons to the New World.

While orange juice will be found on almost every American breakfast table, lemons and limes are used mostly for making cool summer drinks and for flavoring desserts. Grapefruits have nothing in common with grapes except that they grow in clusters on the tree. One tree often produces as much as half a ton of fruit at one time.

A little more than a hundred years ago, the lime made naval history. Crews of British ships, sailing on long voyages and living on meat and biscuits, frequently developed a killing disease known as scurvy. The British didn't know it at the time, but scurvy is caused by vitamin deficiency. Then, by a happy accident, it was discovered that when lime juice was introduced into the sailor's diet, the scurvy disappeared. And so a daily ration of lime juice was thereafter served to every British seaman. To this day, British sailors are sometimes referred to as "Limeys."

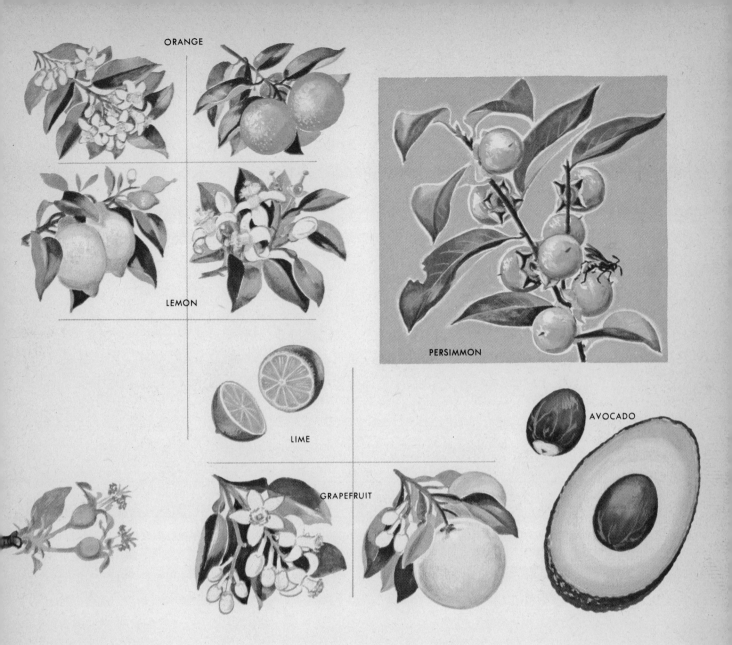

ORANGE

LEMON

PERSIMMON

LIME

AVOCADO

GRAPEFRUIT

The *avocado* is a typically American tropical fruit that was first cultivated and eaten by the Aztec Indians. Unlike other fruits, it cannot be cooked, canned, or otherwise preserved. It must be eaten fresh, usually in a salad.

You can make an interesting experiment with the large plum-size seed of the avocado. If you place the seed in a jar of water, it will soon put out roots and a small delicate stem. In a few weeks, the stem will develop leaves. Pot it, and after several months you will have a handsome little tropical tree, a foot or more high, as an ornament for

your kitchen window. Of course, if you live north of southern California or Florida you cannot plant it outdoors.

THE NUT TREES

Walnuts and *hickories,* the two most common American nut trees are as valuable for their fine woods as for their delicious fruits. Hard, smooth-grained, and nearly splinterless, the wood of the walnut has always been a great favorite for fine cabinet work. Hickory, tough, light and elastic, usually finds its ultimate form in handles for tools. When burned, hickory wood gives off a light,

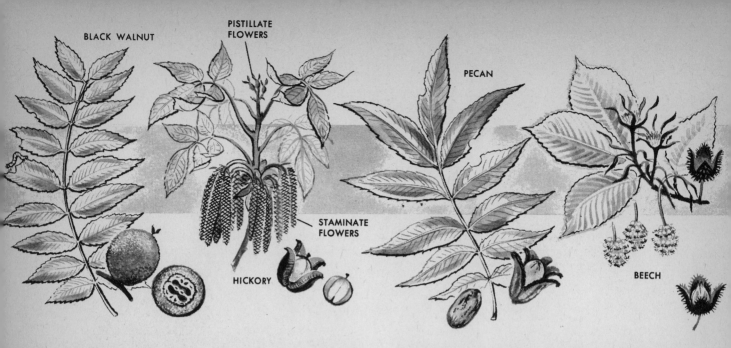

BLACK WALNUT

PISTILLATE FLOWERS

PECAN

STAMINATE FLOWERS

HICKORY

BEECH

flavorful smoke and is used in the South for curing hams and other meats.

The meat of walnuts and hickory nuts is rich in calories and proteins. One of the great old-time outdoor sports, that most children miss in this day of packaged food, is the fun of going out into the woods and gathering up sackfuls of these goodies for the family table.

The husk of the *butternut,* a type of walnut, was used by pioneer families to make a yellowish-brown dye for coloring homespun cloth. During the American Civil War, Confederate soldiers were often called "Butternuts" because their home-made uniforms were dyed with this material.

The *pecan,* which grows wild in the woods of the Deep South, is perhaps the only edible American nut that is cultivated in orchards. In Georgia and Texas, pecan groves are often as large as orange groves. The pecan is the only nut that provides American farmers with a multi-million dollar industry.

The *cashew* (its name is an English corruption of the French word *acajou*) is an evergreen tree that is native to

Central and South America. Today, however, it is chiefly grown in India and Africa. A small tree, between 20 and 40 feet tall, with widely spreading branches, it produces a fruit that resembles an apple in both shape and taste. Appended to the fruit, almost as though Nature did it as an afterthought, is the familiar cashew nut which is so delicious when freshly roasted.

The *Brazil nut,* which is sometimes called the castanea or para nut, is the fruit of a giant hardwood tree that grows wild in the Amazon jungle. It has huge, foot-long leaves and clusters of delicate cream-colored flowers.

The fruit is a hard shell, about the size of a cantaloupe, inside of which are a dozen or more triangular-shaped nuts. The fruits are collected by Brazilian Indians, and shipped mostly to the United States. The meat of the nut is oily and rich, and — besides being eaten — is sometimes pressed into oil that is used for lubricating watches and other delicate machinery.

The *horsechestnut* is a big, handsome tree which people in the Midwest plant around their homes for shade. The

CASHEW

BUCKEYE

BRAZIL NUT

HAZEL NUT

leaves grow in clusters of five or seven, and spread out like the fingers of an open hand.

The large nuts, which are encased in thorny burrs, are dark brown with a white spot at the base, which makes them resemble the eye of a deer. This fact gives the buckeye, a variety of horsechestnut, its name. To reverse this naming process, the state of Ohio is called the Buckeye State because so many of these handsome trees abound in Ohio woods and fields. The fruit of the buckeye and horsechestnut looks as though it should be good to eat, but it is bitter and very distasteful. "It's only good enough for horses," the pioneers used to say; and, of course, that is how it got its name.

The *beech* is one of the most beautiful trees in the American woods. Tall and stately, it has a heavy bole and strong, sturdy limbs. Its bark is thin and smooth, and bright silver in color. The leaves, perhaps the most perfectly shaped of those on any tree, glisten a bright, sleek green in the sun. In winter, they turn from green to gold, and most of them stay on the tree until they are

forced off by the spring's new crop. The silvery bark and the golden leaves make one of Nature's prettiest pictures as they gleam like a huge jewel in the winter woods.

The beech doesn't seem to mind growing in the shade, and so it manages to crowd out other trees that need direct sunlight more.

Beechnuts, though very small, are savory and delicious. But squirrels, birds, deer, and other wild woodland creatures enjoy them as much as man does — and these animals generally get first choice.

Beech wood, reddish brown, smooth-grained, and extremely hard and durable, is used chiefly for furniture and wooden bowls.

SOME UNUSUAL AMERICAN TREES.

The *eucalyptus*, a native tree of Australia, has been transplanted to California where it thrives like a giant weed. A big eucalyptus looks something like an immense, fluffy cone of cotton candy. Its leaves, long and thin like the willows, are very aromatic and are pressed to extract *eucalyptus oil*, a soothing medication for irritated nose and throat. The branches droop down and the bark is constantly peeling. Next to the sequoia and Douglas fir, the eucalyptus, which often grows to 200 feet high, is one of the tallest trees that grows in America.

The *ailanthus*, which the Chinese called the Tree of Heaven, was imported from that country in the hope of using it as food for American silkworms. The silkworms did not like the ailanthus but the ailanthus liked America, and it began growing and spreading like a weed in moist locations. It thrives in the hard-packed cement city yards and vacant lots, undisturbed by dirt, smoke and insects. The leaves are compound and fernlike. They have from 15-30 leaflets with a scent gland at the base which, when crushed, gives off an offensive odor. The seeds, shaped like an airplane propeller, sail merrily over backyard fences to swell the ailanthus population next door.

The *saguaro*, a cactus-like desert tree, looks like a giant hand with extended fingers because of its tall, often 50 feet high, trunk and up-curving branches. It is called by some people the *candelabra tree*, because its form also suggests a huge candlestick. Having thorny spines instead of leaves, the chlorophyll is contained in its tough skin covering.

The *Joshua tree*, related to the palms and another product of the desert, has been called the "ugliest tree in the world." It grows to a height of 20 to 30 feet. Its trunk and branches are covered with a heavy shaggy bark. The Joshua produces lovely ivory-white blossoms as if to say to the world, "I can't be all bad."

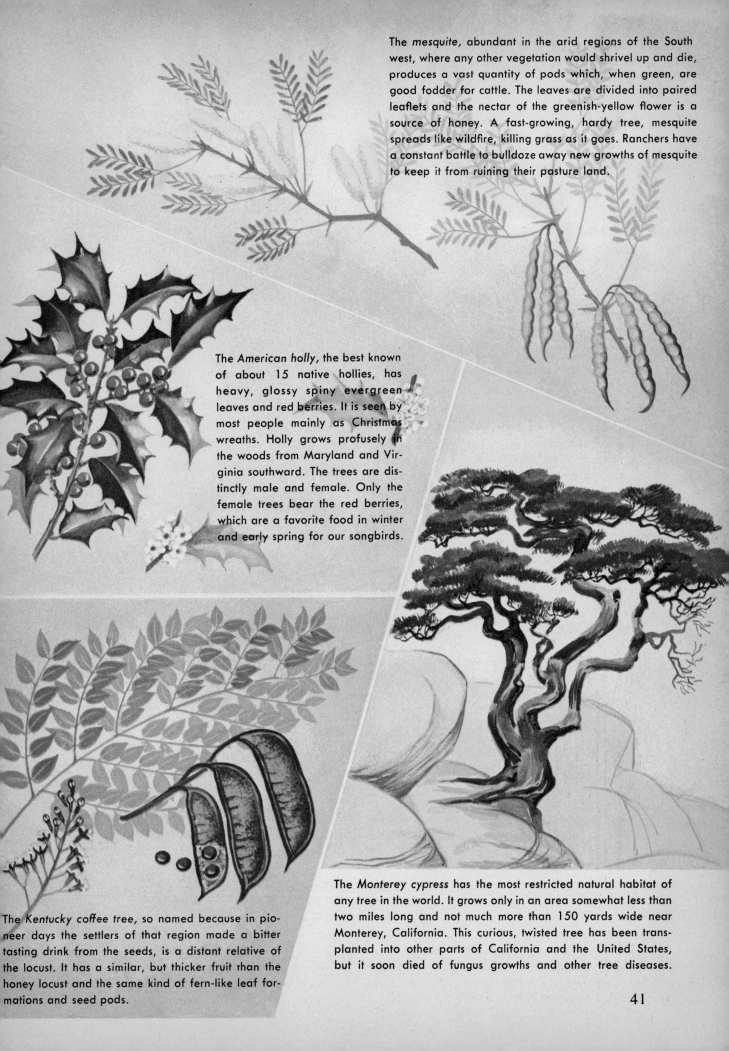

The *mesquite*, abundant in the arid regions of the South west, where any other vegetation would shrivel up and die, produces a vast quantity of pods which, when green, are good fodder for cattle. The leaves are divided into paired leaflets and the nectar of the greenish-yellow flower is a source of honey. A fast-growing, hardy tree, mesquite spreads like wildfire, killing grass as it goes. Ranchers have a constant battle to bulldoze away new growths of mesquite to keep it from ruining their pasture land.

The *American holly*, the best known of about 15 native hollies, has heavy, glossy spiny evergreen leaves and red berries. It is seen by most people mainly as Christmas wreaths. Holly grows profusely in the woods from Maryland and Virginia southward. The trees are distinctly male and female. Only the female trees bear the red berries, which are a favorite food in winter and early spring for our songbirds.

The *Kentucky coffee tree*, so named because in pioneer days the settlers of that region made a bitter tasting drink from the seeds, is a distant relative of the locust. It has a similar, but thicker fruit than the honey locust and the same kind of fern-like leaf formations and seed pods.

The *Monterey cypress* has the most restricted natural habitat of any tree in the world. It grows only in an area somewhat less than two miles long and not much more than 150 yards wide near Monterey, California. This curious, twisted tree has been transplanted into other parts of California and the United States, but it soon died of fungus growths and other tree diseases.

41

Trees of the Tropics

By far the greatest variety of trees, and the strangest ones too, is found in the lush, warm tropical climate. In the jungles of South America, Africa, and Asia, the torrential rains and the broiling sun combine to create a vast natural greenhouse in which all sorts of vegetation wage an eternal fight with each other in a mad scramble for survival. The tall trees, because they can reach their heads up out of the timeless twilight of the jungle floor, are always the winners.

On the dry deserts and broad plains of equatorial Africa, trees take on many unusual forms in Nature's endless effort to adapt them to their surroundings.

Of all tropical trees, the most plentiful and most important commercially is the *coconut palm.* Although it grows all around the world, in a tropical belt from the West Indies to the East Indies, this graceful tree plays its most important role as the key to the economy of the islands of the South Pacific.

In these islands, it furnishes the native with nearly all the necessities of living. Its trunk gives him wood for his houses and his canoes. He weaves its broad leaves into roofing material and mats for his floors. Its fruit is his main source of vegetable food, and the hard, brown coconut shells serve him as ladles and dishes. But, most significant of all, the coconut palm is the islands' chief source of export revenue.

The meat of the coconut is rich in vegetable oil. When sun-dried for shipment, it is known commercially as copra, from the Malay word *koppara,* meaning coconut. The United States alone imports hundreds of tons of copra each year as a base for margarine, cooking oils, and soap products.

The *date palm* is the classic tree that adorns the oases of the Saraha Desert. Wherever a spring of water wells up in the desert wastes, there you will find a grove of date palms. The wealth of an Arab who lives on an oasis is judged not by the amount of land he owns but by the number of his palm trees.

Originally a native of Africa, the date palm was introduced in ancient times into Asia and the southern European countries bordering on the Mediterranean Sea. It was brought to California many years ago by missionaries, where it has become an important fruit crop.

The *banana* is not a true tree at all, but rather a tree-like plant that grows to small-tree size. It is the main staple of food for many tribes of the African jungle, and is grown commercially in West Africa, Central and South America, and the West Indies.

The *breadfruit,* another of the chief food items of the South Sea islands that come from trees, tastes like fresh bread when it is roasted in its shell.

The famous "mutiny on the *Bounty"* was directly caused by breadfruit trees. Captain Bligh and his ship had been dispatched to Tahiti to collect breadfruit seedlings. His mission was to take them to the English colonies in the West Indies for transplanting. On the way, however, water supplies on the *Bounty* began to run low. In order to water his precious seedlings, Bligh denied water to the crew. This caused the crew to mutiny, set Captain Bligh and most of his officers adrift in an open boat, and eventually establish a colony of their own on remote Pitcairn Island.

The *traveler's tree*, which grows on the dry plains of central Africa is as prettily shaped as a palm-leaf fan. A hole bored in its trunk at the base of the fan will give up a pint or more of clear, fresh water. This exotic-looking tree, which can be discerned for long distances on the level plain, has thus saved many a traveler from dying of thirst on the arid veldt. And this, of course, is how it got its name.

Without doubt, the strangest-looking tree in the world is the *baobab*, a native of Africa. A native legend says that a giant child of the gods once pulled up a tree by the roots and then stuck it back into the ground upside down. This is exactly what the baobab looks like. The entire trunk of this weird tree is a water tank. It will keep a thousand gallons or more of water fresh and sweet for several months.

Although the attempt at transplanting the breadfruit tree from the East Indies to the West Indies was a failure, the transposition of the *rubber* tree — the other way around — was almost too much of a success.

The rubber tree is a native of the Amazon valley. Its seedlings were shipped to Ceylon, Sumatra, and Malaya in the 1880's. There, in completely strange ground, it thrived much better than it had ever done in South America. Today, most of the world's rubber comes from the East Indies.

The *sapodilla*, which grows in Guatemala, is the source of chicle, the basic ingredient of chewing gum. These trees grow wild in the jungle rather than on plantations. Indians roam at random through the forest and tap the trees wherever they find them. Then they take the solidified sap downstream to trading posts by canoe. Oddly enough, the wood of the sapodilla is highly prized as extremely hard and durable timber.

The world's three most popular beverages — coffee, tea, and cocoa — are the products of trees, all of which grow in the tropics.

Originally a native of Africa, *coffee* trees have been planted throughout the Near East as well as in Central and South America. Since too much sun is harmful to the berries, coffee trees are grown in the shade of taller trees and carefully nurtured. Caffeine, an essential chemical ingredient found in coffee, is also used in making cola drinks. Although not as common as the drink it produces, the heavy and smoothly-grained wood of the coffee tree — is used to make fine furniture.

The *tea* tree, sometimes no taller than a shrub, grows chiefly in China and India. Tea was one of the great luxuries in Colonial America. When the British put a tax upon it, the people of Boston staged the notorious Boston Tea Party, in which several shipments of tea were dumped into Boston Harbor as a protest. This was one of the historic events that led to the Revolutionary War.

The next time you drink a cup of hot chocolate or eat a chocolate bar, re-

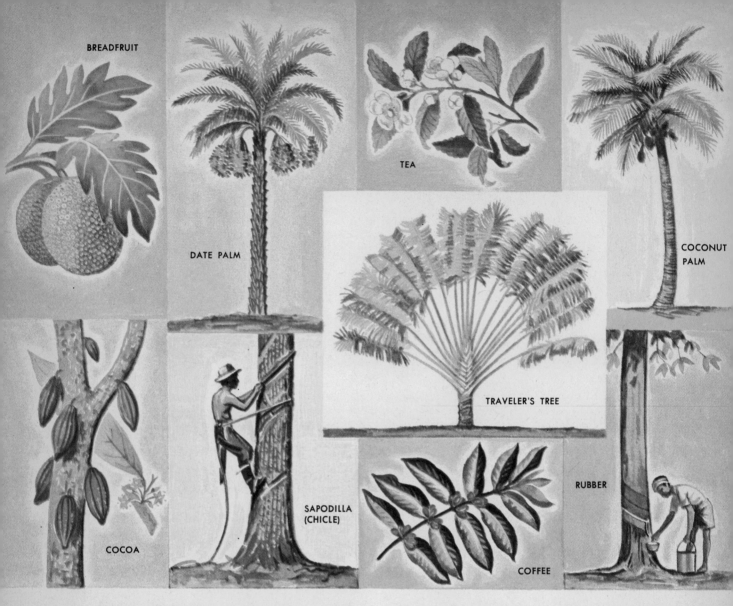

BREADFRUIT

DATE PALM

TEA

COCONUT PALM

COCOA

SAPODILLA (CHICLE)

TRAVELER'S TREE

RUBBER

COFFEE

member that it came from the fruit of a beautiful tropical tree. The *cocoa* tree is another prime example of successful transplantation. It originally grew in Central America. Many years ago, seedlings were introduced into the west coast countries of Africa. There it flourished even better than it had ever done in its native land. Today, most of the world's cocoa comes from Africa. The biggest single exporter is the new Republic of Ghana.

The Medicine Trees

We have seen that the early settlers in America made some of their medicine from trees — the bark of the toothache tree and the roots of the sassafras for example. Two other trees native to the United States are the sources of modern medicinal products.

The *witch hazel* is only a shrub in the Northeast, but in the southern mountains it attains the height of a fair-

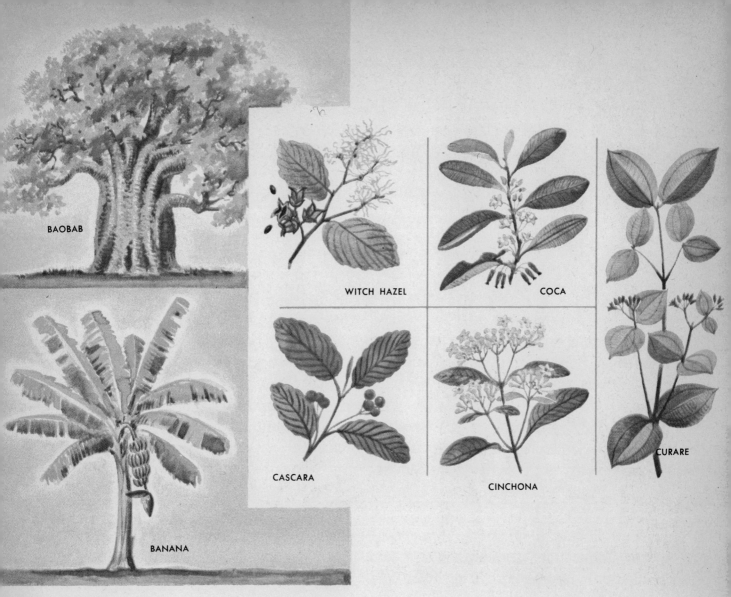

BAOBAB

WITCH HAZEL

COCA

CASCARA

CINCHONA

CURARE

BANANA

sized tree. Its fruits are tough, paper-like containers, each of which holds two little oval-shaped seeds. At the first touch of frost in the fall, these fruits explode like miniature cannons, shooting the seeds out into the air twenty feet or more away. A soothing preparation, distilled from witch hazel bark, is sold in all drugstores for mosquito bites, and minor skin irritations.

The *cascara buckthorn* grows in western Oregon and Washington and nowhere else in the world. A small tree, it is found around the edges of the great forests of Douglas fir. The bark is boiled down to make a commercial laxative medicine called cascara. Stripping the bark unfortunately kills the tree; but the cascara buckthorn grows quickly and prolifically, and there is always a plentiful supply.

A deadly poison is the sap of the *curare* tree, a native of Brazil. Indians tip their arrows in this potent juice or in a gummy resin made from the seeds and can thus kill game or human enemies upon contact. A drug made from curare is used in medicine for controlling muscular spasms.

Two other South American trees yield drugs that have saved many lives and done wonders to control pain.

The leaves of the *coca* tree produce cocaine, a blessing to anyone who has

45

ever had to have a tooth drilled or pulled. The bark of the *cinchona* tree is refined to make quinine, a specific cure for malaria. Until quinine was discovered, malaria annually killed millions of people in tropical countries.

Another tree that was transplanted from South America to the East Indies, cinchona thrived so well in its new surroundings that the islands of Indonesia now produce practically all of the world's quinine supply.

Some Historic Trees

A number of individual trees have become famous in American history. One of these was Connecticut's Charter Oak.

In 1687, King James II wished to take away the charter of the Connecticut Colony. He therefore sent Sir Edmund Andros to Hartford, the colonial capital, to get the charter and assume control of the government. Members of the Connecticut council, however, did not wish to give up their rights, and so they hid the charter in the hollow trunk of an old oak. This venerable tree blew down during a windstorm on August 21, 1856. At the time of its destruction, it was reputed to be nearly 1,000 years old.

When General George Washington assumed command of the Colonial Army, in Cambridge, Mass., in 1775, the ceremony took place under a large elm tree which later became famous as the Cambridge Elm. The old tree lived until 1923. Its growth rings gave its age as 204 years.

Long years after the mountains of the southeastern United States had been settled, a farmer in Tennessee found an old beech tree with this inscription carved into the smooth bark of the trunk:

D. BOON

CILLED A BAR

ON THIS TREE

IN THE YEAR 1760.

Obviously, Dan'l Boone could hunt a lot better than he could spell.

Another beech that figured in an early forest tragedy was found a great many years ago in the mountains of West Virginia. At the base of the tree lay the skeleton of a man, and the rusted remains of a knife and a gun. This verse was carved on the tree:

STRANGE IS MY NAME

AND I'M ON STRANGE GROUND

AND STRANGE IT IS THAT I CAN'T

BE FOUND.

In honor of this unknown pioneer, the little stream that flowed nearby was named Strange Creek.

ACTIVITIES:

There are quite a number of things you can do that will give you lots of fun and at the same time will enable you to study and compare trees more carefully. There are many ways to preserve leaves; you can press them or reproduce them as leaf prints or in plaster casts. You can preserve the flowers, cone seeds and winter twigs, or you can buy and grow your own trees on the window sill.

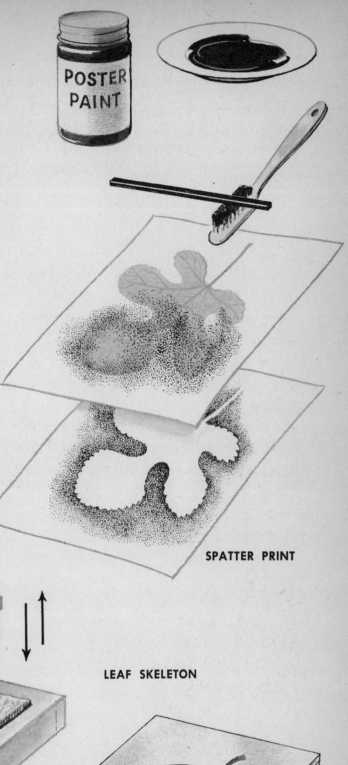

To make a SPATTER PRINT first spread a large piece of paper over your table for protection. Pin a pressed leaf to a sheet of construction paper. Dip an old toothbrush in a dish with poster paint. Take a stick and scrape it through the brush toward you. This will make the bristles of the brush snap back, away from you, and spatter the paint around the leaf. After removing the leaf, a perfect print of it remains on the paper.

To make a LEAF SKELETON which you can mount in a scrap book and preserve, take a fresh, green leaf and put it on a "pounding board." (A piece of old carpet or floor mat on top of a plank will do the trick.)

SPATTER PRINT

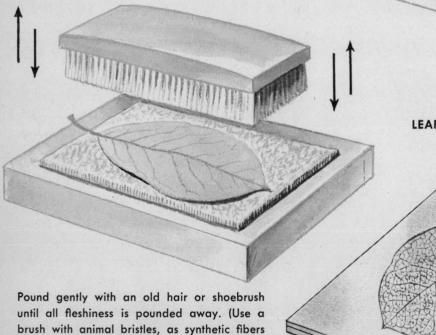

LEAF SKELETON

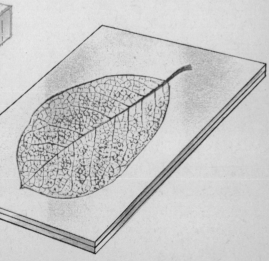

Pound gently with an old hair or shoebrush until all fleshiness is pounded away. (Use a brush with animal bristles, as synthetic fibers are too harsh.) Hold the leaf, top side up, firmly with one hand in place. After a short while, only the beautiful network of veins will remain.

47

It is not too difficult to start a collection of tree seeds, label them and store them in a collection box. But it is even more fun to get the fresh seeds to grow into little trees. Put a layer of pebbles into a flower pot or a glass tank and add sandy soil to within an inch of the top, pressing the soil firmly down. Put your seeds in, cover them slightly with soil and press down again.

Place your pot on the window sill and water with a bulb spray whenever the soil feels dry. Keep it moist, but never really wet. Protect the top of your tree nursery with a pane of glass or a newspaper which you will remove when the seeds start to sprout.

**COLLECTION
OF WINTER TWIGS**

POPLAR
MAPLE
MAGNOLIA
BEECH
BUCKEYE
PAULOWNIA

**COLLECTION
OF TREE SEEDS**

Leaves that you want to mount in your scrap book have to be carefully dried out first. Place each individual leaf between sheets of a folded newspaper. Put some more folded paper on top and underneath the one you use for pressing the leaf and put a weight or heavy books on top of the pile. Keep them this way until the leaf is dried out and pressed flat. Then mount them in your book with identification labels.

48